Table of Contents

INTRODUCTION

The conclusion of the 20th Century witnessed the collapse of the former Soviet Union and marked the end of the cold war. The United States of America has entered the 21st Century as the world's lone global super power militarily and economically. The United States (U.S.) entry into the new century has been marked by the terrorist attacks of September 11th, 2001 and the subsequent U.S. military actions in both Afghanistan and Iraq, as part of the Global War on Terrorism, which is ongoing nearly eight years later.

There is a large debate today in both academic and military communities as to what the right road ahead is for the U.S. and in particular the U.S. military. How should the U.S. military best prepare in order to win the current Global War on Terror and simultaneously position itself to face the unknown threats, future conflicts, and wars it will be required to fight and win throughout the 21st Century? Does the U.S. Military need to possess a strong conventional type military force or is a more unconventional focused, trained, and equipped military force more reflective of what will be required to address and win the conflicts of the future? A large part of the debate focuses on determining what will be the environment and threats of the 21st Century, how should the U.S. Military best prepare for those threats, and are the U.S. Military and the U.S. Government learning the right lessons from the current War on terror to correctly address those perceived future threats.

What is not up for debate is the requirement for the U.S. military to fight and win the future conflicts, battles, and wars that could potentially materialize as the 21st Century continues to unfold. Failure to do so would jeopardize the current U.S. position throughout the world and possibly even the very existence of the U.S. as a free democratic nation. The United States

1

military's success on the battlefields of the 21st Century will require a continued focus on high intensity combat operations (conventional warfare) ensuring the right lessons are learned from the current War on Terror in order to maintain, train, lead, and equip a military capable of winning decisively.

CONTEXT
CONVENTIONAL VS UNCONVENTIONAL WARFARE

In order to understand why it is imperative that the U.S. military remains focused on conventional warfare it is essential to gain an understanding of what conventional warfare is and likewise, what is unconventional warfare. Conventional warfare is not found as a term within Joint Publication 1-02: Doctrine for the Armed Forces of the United States. Joint Publication 1-02 defines the term conventional forces as, "1. Those forces capable of conducting operations using nonnuclear weapons. 2. Those forces other than designated special operations forces."[1] Political Geography Glossary defines conventional warfare as: "Armed conflict between states and/or nations in which combatants appear in organized military units that are often outfitted with standard uniforms, weapons, and equipment. It typically involves major combat operations that overtly seize control of territory, inhabitants, and resources."[2] Unconventional warfare is defined in Joint Publication 1-02 as:

> A broad spectrum of military and paramilitary operations, normally of long duration, predominantly conducted through, with, or by indigenous or surrogate forces who are organized, trained, equipped, supported, and directed in varying degrees by an external source. It includes, but is not limited to, guerilla warfare, subversion, sabotage, intelligence activities, and unconventional assisted recovery.[3]

2

Using the definition of conventional forces that Joint Publication 1-02 (JP 1-02) provides one can logically deduct that conventional warfare encompasses all warfare short of warfare using nuclear weapons and involves those forces not specifically labeled special operating forces.[4] The Political Geography Glossary definition adds further clarification to the term conventional warfare in particular; major combat operations directed at controlling territory, inhabitants and resources.[5] The definition of unconventional warfare as defined by JP 1-02 includes the words military and paramilitary operations but does not utilize the word "combat" anywhere in defining unconventional warfare.[6] Within, *A Tentative Manual For Countering Irregular Threats An Updated Approach to Counterinsurgency,* produced by the United States Marine Corps Combat Development Command it discusses the term irregular warfare stating, "the term irregular is used in the broad, inclusive sense to refer to all types of non-conventional methods of violence employed to counter the traditional capabilities of an opponent."[7] It goes on to further clarify that the term irregular warfare includes both state and non-state participants who desire to drive out or lessen the authority of local or outside governments.[8]

In September of 2005 an Irregular Warfare workshop was convened by the special Operations Command in conjunction with the Assistant Secretary of Defense for Special Operations and Low-Intensity conflict in order to explore and reach consensus as to the appropriate Department of Defense (DOD) definitions for Irregular Warfare and Irregular Operations.[9] The need for a common understanding of the meaning of terms utilized within the Military and other Government agencies is critical to ensure all agencies within government and all services within the DOD have a clear meaning and understanding of terms used. There is an inherent danger, if the very words we use to describe types of warfare and future threats are not commonly understood throughout the whole of government. After probing the current definitions of conventional and unconventional warfare, it is safe to assume that conventional warfare is used to describe warfare as it has been come to be known throughout the 20th Century, short of the use of nuclear weapons and involves high intensity combat. Unconventional and irregular warfare are terms to describe adversaries who seek to conduct war but, choose not to directly engage the U.S. Military in the traditional means through the use of an organized and equipped air force, navy, and army, or employing large ground forces and chooses to employ other means, tactics, and procedures to achieve their objectives.

THE ENVIRONMENT & THREATS OF THE 21st CENTURY

Understanding the possible threats, adversaries, and means in which the U.S. Military could be employed in the future is essential to shaping, equipping, and training the U. S. Military to address those threats. What is not so clear is what those threats will be. Similarly, as it is important to understand possible future threats, it is equally important to acknowledge that even the best analysis of future threats is just that, an analysis. General Makhmut Gareev in his work: *If War Comes tomorrow? The contours of Future Armed conflict* points out that, "History knows of many accurate predictions regarding certain aspects of future wars, but nobody has yet succeeded in foreseeing the nature of any forthcoming armed struggles in their totality."[10] One only has to look at the 20th Century to see how difficult it is to predict what the next conflict, war, or use of military force will be. World War I (WWI) was believed to be a war that would end all wars and at its conclusion in 1918, few anticipated that World War II (WWII) would be fought just over two decades later.[11] Post WWII, few predicted the cold war that would follow between the U.S. and the Soviet Union when in 1945 and 1946 large numbers

4

of U.S. forces were brought back to the U.S. and the U.S. military began to demobilize.[12] Shortly following WWII, although there was intelligence reporting indicating that the North Korean People's Army might be preparing for an offensive into South Korea, few believed that an attack was approaching.[13] Attempting to anticipate the future conflicts of the 21st Century is a necessary endeavor to best build, train and equip a military for the possible unknowns. However, before continuing to look at the perceived threats of the 21st Century we must recognize that history teaches us we have often been surprised.

The 2008 U.S. National Defense Strategy (NDS) describes a future strategic environment that will be defined by global conflict versus violent ideological extremists, both state and non-state actors, that will seek the use of weapons of mass destruction and possibly threaten the existence of the international state system[14] It further states, "Over the next twenty years physical pressures – population, resource, energy, climatic and environmental – could combine with rapid social, cultural, technological and geopolitical change to create greater uncertainty."[15] The United States Marine Corps' *Vision & Strategy 2025*, describes a similar environment in which, future adversaries, both state and non-state actors, will improve their lethal capabilities and chose to engage their opponents in both a conventional and unconventional manner, often jumping between the two distinctions of warfare utilizing what has recently been termed hybrid warfare.[16] *Vision & Strategy 2025 states*, "Hybrid conflicts are assessed as the most likely form of conflict facing the United States."[17] This new type of warfare is expected to unfold in the 21st Century due to the U.S. military's current dominance in waging conventional warfare. It is believed that future adversaries will seek other military (hybrid) means to achieve their desired military and political objectives.[18] Current U.S. Army Chief of Staff, Gen. George W. Casey further expounded on the future threat environment when making remarks at the National Press club he said, "We are going to face a period of protracted global confrontation among state, non-state and individual actors who will increasingly use violence as a means of achieving their political and ideological objectives."[19] There appears to be a consensus among military and governmental senior leadership as to the likely anticipated threats the U.S. Military can expect to face as the U.S. continues to move forward into the 21st Century. One wonders, then what the likelihood is of future adversaries conducting conventional warfare in the 21st Century particularly as defined by the Political Geography Glossary, "… typically involves major combat operations that overtly seize control of territory, inhabitants, and resources."[20]

One does not have to look a long way into the future to identify possible areas and circumstances existing today where the potential for future conventional warfare exists. Countries such as China, North Korea, Russia, and Iran all pose separate but credible conventional threats globally and regionally. As described in the U.S. Department of Defense's, annual report to Congress, *Military Power of the People's Republic of China 2007*, the Chinese government continues to modernize and expand their military capabilities, "The expanding military capabilities of China's armed forces are a major factor in changing East Asian military balances; improvements in China's strategic capabilities have ramifications far beyond the Asian Pacific region."[21] Recent Russian aggression in Georgia, the continued stand-off on the Korean Peninsula, and the spreading Iranian influence throughout the Middle East all are potential future flashpoints that could possibly require a large U.S. conventional military force reaction.

The Department of Defense's *NDS 2008*, the Marine Corps' *Vision and Strategy 2025* and *A Tentative Manual For Countering Irregular Threats, An Updated Approach to*

Counterinsurgency all describe in detail the anticipated environment and threats of the 21st Century. They describe an environment similar to the past, but also very different which will require a new focus for the U.S. Military in order to address the environment and threats anticipated in the future. Each document makes mention of a requirement for U.S. Military forces to retain their current dominance in conventional warfare however, the focus is not placed on conventional warfare capabilities. The difficult task becomes the ability to maintain the much needed conventional capabilities and skills and at the same time being able to adapt and modifying to new dynamic environments and threats. The danger lies in adapting to such a degree that conventional capabilities atrophy and as a military we are unable to respond to high intensity combat operations as effectively as we currently can. The need to retain the conventional warfighting edge and remain strongly focused on training, leading, and equipping a military to wage conventional warfare is paramount to the U.S. Military as it faces the challenges of the current war on Terror and future threats of the 21st Century.

In Geoffrey Blainey's work, *The Causes of War*, he discusses that over the past 1,000 years Russia has had only one quarter of peace within any century and that in every other period spanning 25 years Russia has been engaged in some type of war.[22] Likewise he points out that England, "…since the time of William the Conqueror, had been engaged in war somewhere in Europe or the tropics for 56 of each hundred years."[23] Few disagree that the 21st Century will be complex, changing, and violent. When looking at the possible future environment and threats of the 21st Century and discussing varying types of warfare it is critical for the U.S. military to remain focused on the fundamentals of what war is. Marine Corps Doctrinal Publication 1 describes war as, "… a violent clash of interests between or among organized groups characterized by the use of military force."[24] This definition of war encompasses conventional, unconventional, irregular, and hybrid types of warfare. The danger to be avoided for the U.S. military as it continues into the 21st Century is twofold. First, it must not solely subscribe to any one type of warfare that does not incorporate the others and account for the most dangerous possible future threats. Secondly, it must remain focused on the primary role of any military...winning wars. This sounds obvious, but during times of change every effort needs to be made that the changes occurring are the right changes, driven by the right reasons. Changes are necessary to adapt to an ever changing environment and set of enemy threats however, second and third order affects of any change must be carefully scrutinized.

CURRENT DEBATE ON HOW BEST TO PREPARE THE U.S. MILITARY FOR THE ENVIRONMENT AND THREATS OF THE 21ST CENTURY

As the debate unfolds as to what the environment and threats of the 21st Century will be, a concurrent debate is carried on about how the U.S. Military should best prepare to face the threats and anticipated environment of the future. The debate largely focuses on how the U.S. Department of Defense and the U.S. military should transform in order to address, not only winning the current War on Terror, but how to best structure, train, and equip the U.S. military for the possible future conflicts of the 21st Century. The debate can be classified generally around three separate schools of thought. The first is a belief that the U.S. military needs a complete transformation in order to effectively win the War on Terror and be able to confront the threats of the 21st Century. The second belief is that the U.S. military must be able to conduct operations across the full spectrum of conflicts; conventional, unconventional, irregular, hybrid, and do all equally as well. Third, the views that the U.S. Military must remain dominate in the area of conventional warfare to best protect the U.S. interests and win the wars of the 21st Century.

The Commandant of the U.S. Marine Corps, Gen. James T. Conway describes a Marine Corps, in *Marine Corps Vision & Strategy 2025*, that will, "serve credibly as a persistently engaged and multi capable force, able to draw upon contributions from our Total Force, in order to address the full range of contingencies the future will undoubtedly present.[25] The United States Marine Corps has a long history of being a flexible expeditionary force that the U.S. has employed in both "large" and "small" wars and of all the services within the DOD is arguably most prepared for the current and future operating environment from a historical perspective. The NDS 2008 discusses the need for these same types of capabilities when it states, "When called upon, the Department must be positioned to defeat enemies employing a combination of capabilities, conventional and irregular, kinetic and non-kinetic, across the spectrum of conflict."[26]

Michael Melillo in his article, *Outfitting a Big-War Military with Small-War Capabilities*, argues that the U.S. Military has been overly focused on conventional warfare since the ending of the cold war, despite recent unconventional conflicts involving the U.S. in places such as Somalia and Bosnia and past conflicts in Vietnam and Beirut.[27] As a result, the Department of Defense and U.S. Military were slow to react to the asymmetrical threat posed by adversaries globally and within Iraq and is having a hard time fighting a "Small-War" with a "Big-War" military.[28] Difficulty addressing the Small-War, as Michael Melillo describes, does not necessarily draw the conclusion that the "Big-War" military needs a drastic change especially, considering the additional threats likely and "unlikely" to appear in the future. At first glance yes, the U.S. military has been combating an insurgency for some time. However, historically

9

counter-insurgencies are often long in duration and do not tend to have immediately obtainable objectives (as is normally associated with conventional warfare) that bring about a quick decisive victory. Michael Melillo continues to say in his article, "the American military must be capable of thriving across the entire spectrum of conflict, from the large, conventional conflicts it prefers to the irregular small wars that are prevalent today."[29] Secretary Gates speaking at the Association of the United States Army annual meeting and exposition stated, "It strikes me that one of the principal challenges the Army faces is to regain its traditional edge at fighting conventional wars while retaining what it has learned and relearned about unconventional wars, the ones most likely to be fought in the years ahead."[30]

The U.S. Military clearly needs a lethal, flexible, versatile force that can operate not only at the high end of intense combat operations (conventionally), but can quickly adjust to lower intensity situations and missions. The difficult portion of how best to modify and prepare the military for the future lies in "the what" and "the how" to adjust in order to create that more well-rounded force and how does that force become altered without losing precious proficiency in the conventional warfighting skills. Ensuring the U.S. possesses the right balanced military force to address the current and future threat is paramount to U.S. National Interests both now and in the future. Lessons learned from the War on Terror are significantly important in driving the direction and pace of the current military transformation. Drawing the correct lessons learned from the current War on Terror are imperative to winning the war, as well as, forging a solid road ahead for the U.S. Military into the 21st Century. Ensuring the right lessons learned are reflected in the changes across the U.S. Government and Military is critical to the long term success of the U.S.

ARE WE LEARNING THE RIGHT LESSONS LEARNED FROM THE CURRENT WAR ON TERROR?

The lessons being learned in regards to the War on terror are major instruments in driving the changes in tactics, techniques, and procedures currently underway within the U.S. Military to address and counter ever evolving enemy threats. The preponderance of lessons learned has come from Iraq, due to the level and duration of U.S. Forces involvement there. The U.S. government and Military have learned invaluable lessons that have already affected the U.S. Military's training, equipment acquisitions, doctrine, and employment. As the U.S. Military makes transformational changes in response to lessons learned from the War on Terror, it is important to analyze and understand what changes are occurring currently within the military and how will that affect the U.S. Military's conventional capabilities long term within the 21st Century.

With the development of an insurgency in Iraq, the U.S. Military has responded with aggressive measures to train, equip, and provide updated doctrine to U.S. Military personnel to carry out and win the counterinsurgency underway. The recent publication of *Field Manual 3-24/ MCWP 3-33.5 COUNTERINSURGENCY* and documents such as *Through the Lens of Cultural Awareness: A Primer for US Armed Forces Deploying to Arab and Middle Eastern Countries* are examples of doctrine development directed at educating and training U.S. Forces at all levels for counterinsurgency operations. Tactics, techniques, and procedures to counter IEDs and other enemy actions are quickly captured and disseminated throughout the force. Secretary of Defense, Robert Gates, in a recent article said that, "In Iraq, we have seen how an army that was basically a small version of the Cold War Force can become an effective instrument of counterinsurgency over time."[31] Clearly the Lessons being learned by the U.S.

Military at the tactical and operational level of war are enabling the U.S. Military forces to defeat the insurgency and are setting the conditions for long term success in Iraq. However, what strategic lessons have we learned at the U.S. National level and are those lessons being most advantageously incorporated into the changes currently affecting the U.S. Military as modifications to the U.S. Military are made and considered in order to address the environment and threats still to be faced in the 21st Century?

One of the significant lessons learned during Operation Iraqi Freedom for both the U.S. Government and Military was the initial failure of Phase IV, Stability Operations once the U.S. Military had completed offensive combat operations. The lack of detailed planning associated with post combat hostilities has been the subject of much discussion. U.S. Military leadership and planners were heavily focused with deploying the military force forward into theatre and on the planning that would involve subsequent offensive operations.[32] There also was confusion within the U.S. government as to who had planning responsibility for Phase IV Operations, was it the responsibility of the U.S. Military or was it to be handled by other elements of the U.S. Government?[33] This break down of integrated planning within the U.S. government surrounding Phase IV Operations coupled with decisions made during Phase IV to disband the Iraqi Army contributed to creating an environment in which an insurgency could and did eventually develop.[34] The obvious lesson to be learned here is that planning for all aspects of a campaign must be detailed, complete, and specific responsibilities need to be clearly delineated throughout the Government, that is fairly obvious. The other, not so obvious lesson to be learned, is that as we seek to transform the U.S. military and debate how best to restructure, equip, and train a military for the 21st Century we must be careful not to reshape the military so extensively (at the cost of conventional capability) based on lessons learned as it relates to

Phase IV Operations in Iraq and the insurgency that followed. Those lessons learned are critical, but do not necessarily require a drastic transformation in the U.S. military. As stated earlier, the U.S. military has proven extremely adaptable; fighting a conventional war at the outset of Operation Iraqi Freedom and quickly modifying and adapting training, equipment, tactics, and procedures, while in combat, to engage and defeat a large scale insurgency. The U.S. military has demonstrated its ability to operate across the full spectrum of conflict, which is necessary to win the War on Terror, and is a desired capability to best address possible future conflicts.

As mentioned previously, a lack of detailed planning and confusion within the U.S. government as to the responsibilities for Phase IV planning played a role in the insurgency that developed in Iraq. The examples of Post WWII German and Japanese reconstruction provide examples where the U.S. Government and Military, for the first time, conducted large scale post-conflict nation building where no insurgency developed. In large part, this was the result of extensive planning and key strategic decisions by military and civilian leadership. Prior planning was conducted before the conclusion of WWII by the U.S. Government and in particular the U.S. Military. Before the end of WWII U.S. Military leaders had already begun planning and developing doctrine dealing with civil administration in occupied territories and military government, producing Field Manual (FM) 27-10. "The Rules of Land Warfare" and FM 27-5, "Military Government".[35] In the case of Japanese Reconstruction, key decisions such as retaining the former government and utilizing the former military to facilitate demobilization of the Japanese Military were instrumental in easing the post conflict stability period and reducing the threat of an insurgency developing.[36] In both the occupation of Germany and Japan large numbers of U.S. Military personnel were available, post hostilities, to provide needed security throughout reconstruction. Lessons learned from the successful occupations and reconstruction efforts in Germany and Japan coupled with the lessons learned from post Operation Iraqi Freedom and the subsequent insurgency that developed should draw our attention, not only to the U.S. military which played a significant role and will do so in the future, but also to U.S. Civilian Governmental roles. What role particularly, as we transform and reshape the U.S. Military with the likelihood of having to conduct stability operations and encountering new threats in an uncertain 21st Century should elements of the U.S. Civilian Government play?

THE US MILITARY AND CIVILIAN ELEMENTS OF THE US GOVERNMENT AS IT RELATES TO THE ENVIRONMENT AND THREATS OF THE 21ST CENTURY

As has previously been mentioned, a large portion of the current debate to transform the U.S. Military into a force that will be better able to confront both the environment and threats of the 21st Century is derived from lessons learned from The War on Terror and Iraq in particular. The U.S. Military must remain flexible to adapt to changing situations as it has done in the past and will be required to do so in the future in order to maintain relevance and effectiveness across the spectrum of conflicts. It is not solely a question of whether or not the U.S. military needs to change to address future conflicts; rather it is a question of what changes are necessary throughout the U.S. government as a whole, and what will be the implications of those changes. Specifically, as it relates to the U.S. military's ability to train, lead, and equip a military capable of continued conventional warfare dominance, (high intensity combat operations) in the 21st Century.

14

The U.S. government and military fully anticipate the need to conduct stability and security operations in the future. In a recent article from Foreign Affairs Magazine, U.S. Secretary of Defense, Robert Gates stated, "Whether in the midst of or in the aftermath of any major conflict the requirement for the U.S. military to maintain security, provide aid and comfort, begin reconstruction, and prop up local governments and public services will not go away." [37] Secretary Gates went on to describe a gap that currently exists in the U.S. civilian government national security capability, discussing how the U.S. Agency for International Development (USAID), which had 15,000 employees during the Vietnam timeframe now employs less than 3,000.[38] He adds that since the attacks of September 11th 2001 resources, largely funding and personnel, have been increased within the State Department (The USAID falls within the U.S. State Department) to address capability shortfalls.[39] David Kilcullen in his article, *New Paradigms for the 20th Century Conflict*, points out that the U.S. military has roughly 1.68 million employees in uniform, while the U.S. State Department has approximately 6,000 Foreign Service Officers.[40] He states, "...there are substantially more people employed as musicians in Defense bands than in the entire foreign service."[41]

Both the U.S. military and U.S. civilian government have a role to play as the U.S. faces the environments and threats of the 21st Century. A transformation in the U.S. civilian governmental agencies ability to support future stability operations that would require diplomacy, the providing of essential services, promotion of governance, and economic development would lessen the burden, currently shouldered mostly by the U.S. military. This would allow the U.S. military valuable time and resources to devote to training focused on the high intensity combat operations inherent with conventional warfare. It is not a question of "us" or "them"; it is a question of team work, balance, and a National level of organization and capabilities to sufficiently address the likely scenarios of the 21st Century. Failure to increase

the capabilities of other agencies and instruments of national power throughout the U.S.

Government could in the future place the U.S. military "on a slippery slope" where the

conventional warfighting dominance, currently enjoyed by the U.S. military has been lost.

Other agencies within the U.S. government can be significantly re-organized and given the

resources to take a larger role in future conflicts requiring stability, governance, economic

assistance, etc. However, no other U.S. government agency is capable of winning the high

intense conventional combat confrontations of the future.

In 1996, The National Defense University's Center for Advanced Concepts and

Technology (ACT), published a report titled, *Interagency and Political-Military dimensions of*

Peace Operations: Haiti- A Case Study, in this report the ACT discusses their involvement and

lessons learned from Operation Restore Democracy. The ACT report points out a need for

interagency planning doctrine, discusses the differences in military and interagency planning

capabilities, expresses a lack of civilian agency manpower, identifies the need for established

interagency and military command and control relationships, and describes that there exists an

overall need for military and interagency partnership to accomplish the mission.[42] This report

captures lessons learned regarding the need for military and interagency cooperation to

accomplish stability and security missions over a decade ago and is still as prevalent, if not

more so, today. Today the U.S. military carries much of the responsibility for stability and

security operations. A balanced U.S. government approach, utilizing all the instruments of

national and civilian power, to address future stability and security missions will increase the

likelihood of successful mission accomplishment. In addition, this would enable the U.S.

military greater flexibility to train, lead, and equip a military better able to maintain the skill sets

16

necessary to decisively win the conventional fights of the future, as it has demonstrated the ability to do in recent history, and which, is so critical to U.S. National Security.

MAINTAINING THE CONVENTIONAL EDGE IN THE 21ST CENTURY

Few dispute the fact that conventional warfare will be evident throughout the 21st Century. There is more discussion and debate as to how prevalent will conventional warfare be throughout the century. As the U.S. government continues to move into the 21st Century faced with a challenging environment and multiple threats yet to encounter, maintaining conventional dominance will require time, energy, resources, and a warfighting ethos that must be learned and cultivated.

U.S. Secretary of Defense, Robert Gates, in an article titled, *A Balanced Strategy: Reprogramming the Pentagon for a New Age*, in Foreign Affairs Magazine, discussed how the U. S. would be challenged to fight a conventional ground war with little warning; however, he believed that the U.S. maintained sufficient Air and Naval power to address potential possible threats if necessary.[43]Recent lessons learned taken from the 2006 Hezbollah-Israeli war point to the fact that Israel had an inflated view of air power capabilities to achieve their operational and strategic objectives versus Hezbollah.[44] Sarah Kreps, in *Parameters* Journal states, "…Israel military and civilian leaders seem to have been seduced by the idea that airpower generally and strategic bombing specifically could antiseptically win wars and therefore made land warfare "anachronistic.""[45] Also writing about the 2006 Hezbollah-Israeli War, Matt Matthews in his paper, *We Were Caught Unprepared: The 2006 Hezbollah-Israeli War*, discusses how the Israeli's strategic end state was the destruction of Hezbollah through the integrated use of air power and precision based weapons, but they were unable to destroy Hezbollah with air power alone.[46] Matt Matthews further makes the points that the Israeli Defense forces were not prepared or as effective as was expected throughout the limited ground portions of the war. He states that, "After years of conducting successful counterinsurgency operations against the Palestinians, the Israeli military encountered substantial problems in shifting its focus to major combat operations against Hezbollah."[47] Israeli forces were deficient in conventional tactical warfighting skills such as, utilization of combined arms and possessing the ability to call for indirect fire.[48] The Israeli military encountered a well armed, organized, Hezbollah force. Matthews states, "By the summer of 2006, Hezbollah had assembled a well-trained, well armed, highly motivated, and highly evolved warfighting machine on Israel's northern border.[49] The Israeli lessons learned from the recent 2006 Hezbollah- Israeli War clearly point to a continued need for conventional capabilities able to incorporate air, naval, and ground forces to achieve decisive combat results.

The skill sets, knowledge, and expertise required to integrate air, naval, and ground forces to fight and win conventionally must be continually trained to and maintained. The U.S. military must remain focused on conventional warfare, not to the exclusion of all else, but must not allow a degradation in capabilities to occur which could jeopardize future U.S. Security. No one within the U.S. military or U.S. government member wants that to happen. However; with ever competing demands for time and resources, combined with the U.S. military's significant role as a key instrument of nation power and the current counterinsurgency fight in Iraq on going, every effort must be made to retain a military with the ability to effectively close with and destroy when needed.

CONCLUSION

General Makhmut Gareev, in his book, *If War Comes Tomorrow? The Contours of Future Armed Conflict*, articulates the significance of a U.S. Military able to dominate across the spectrum of warfare when he says:

> Why is the USA taken into account all over the world, why are its interests extending so far, when no other state can afford to do likewise? This is not explained by any specific qualities or intentions of these countries' leaders, but by only one circumstance – The USA is the most powerful state in economic and military respects. And all nations need to take this fact into account, and draw appropriate conclusions from it.[50]

The environments and threats of the 21st Century will be complex, violent, and will force the U.S. military and government to face old and new challenges. Within the academic, military, and governmental areas throughout the U.S. a debate is being conducted as to how the U.S. military should prepare to face the uncertain and challenging road ahead. History teaches us this is not a new debate. The current War on Terror is one that must be won. At the same time, the war in Iraq is teaching valuable lessons learned at the tactical, operational, and strategic levels of war. Adjustments and changes must be made within the U.S. government to reflect the lessons being learned and create new capabilities for possible conflicts across the spectrum of warfare as envisioned in the 21st Century. The U.S. Military and other U.S. government agencies must be flexible to work together in order to employ all the instruments of national power congruently to achieve the national strategic objectives.

The U.S. military must remain focused and grounded in conventional warfare. The lessons learned from the recent Hezbollah-Israeli War demonstrate that overly focusing on any one aspect of warfare will have an effect on a military forces ability to be efficient in another. Unconventional warfare, irregular warfare, informational warfare, and hybrid types of warfare all have importance and must not be ignored. As the U.S. military has demonstrated in carrying out the counterinsurgency in Iraq, the ability to change and adapt tactics, techniques, and procedures to an ever changing enemy is a requirement necessary for any credible military. The danger lies in losing the skills, knowledge, expertise, and warrior culture necessary to dominate conventionally. Maintaining the advantage in conventional warfare will lay the foundation for success across the entire spectrum of Warfare. The U.S. militaries success and in large part the success of the U.S. relies on a military flexible to deal with future unknowns, but grounded in the basics of conventional warfare in order to win decisively as it has in the past and might be required to do again in the future.

[1] U.S. Department of Defense, *Joint Publication 1-02: Department of Defense Dictionary of Military and Associated Terms* (Washington D.C: U.S. Department of Defense, October 17, 2008), 124. http: // www . dtic . mil / doctrine / jel / new _ pubs / jpl_ 02.pdf (Accessed January 17, 2009)

[2] Political Geography Glossary. http://www.umsl.edu / ~ naumannj / geog%202001%20glossaries / political%20geographyh / POLITICALL%20GEOGRAPHY%20GLOSSARY.doc (accessed January 13, 2009)

[3] *Joint Publication 1-02: Department of Defense Dictionary of Military and Associated Terms*, 547.

[4] *Joint Publication 1-02: Department of Defense Dictionary of Military and Associated Terms*, 124.

[5] Political Geography Glossary. http://www.umsl.edu / ~ naumannj / geog%202001%20glossaries / political%20geographyh / POLITICALL%20GEOGRAPHY%20GLOSSARY.doc (accessed January 13, 2009)

[6] *Joint Publication 1-02: Department of Defense Dictionary of Military and Associated Terms*, 547.

[7] Marine Corps Combat Development Command, *A Tentative Manual For Countering Irregular Threats An Updated Approach TO Counterinsurgency* (Quantico, V.A: U.S. Marine Corps, June 07, 2006), 1

[8] *A Tentative Manual For Countering Irregular Threats An Updated Approach to Counterinsurgency*, 7.

[9] The U.S. Special Operations Command and Assistant Secretary of Defense for Special Operations and Low-Intensity Conflict, *Summary of Irregular Warfare Workshop*, September 20, 2005, http:// smallwars.quantico . usmc. mil / search / articles / Summary of Irregular Warfare Workshop.pdf (accessed January 14, 2009)

[10] General Makhmut Gareev, *If War Comes tomorrow? The Contours of Future Armed Conflict* (London: Frank Cass Publishers,1998),vii.

[11] J.A.S. Grenville, *A History Of The World in the twentieth Century* (Massachusetts: The Belknap Press of Harvard University Press, 1994), 9, 251.

[12] J.A.S. Grenville, 372.

[13] Roy E. Appleman, *United States Army In the Korean War South To The Naktong, North To The Yalu* (Washington, D.C: Center of Military History United States Army, 1992), 20-21.

[14] United States Department of Defense, *2008 National Defense Strategy* (Washington D.C: Department of Defense, 2008),2, http://www. defenselink . mil / news / 2008%20national%20defense%strategy.pdf (accessed January 15, 2009)

[15] United States Department of Defense, *2008 National Defense Strategy*, 4.

[16] Headquarters U.S. Marine Corps, *Marine Corps vision & Strategy 2025* (Washington D.C: U.S. Marine Corps),19-23.

[17] Headquarters U.S. Marine Corps, *Marine Corps vision & Strategy 2025*, 21.

[18] Headquarters U.S. Marine Corps, *Marine Corps vision & Strategy 2025*, 21-22.

[19] George W.Casey, "U.S. Army Prepares for Future Conflicts," *Military Technology*, Vol. 31 (October 2007): 18-21, http:// proquest . umi . com / pqdweb?did=1384477361&Fmt=3&clientId=32176&RQT=309&VName=PQD (accessed October 23, 2008)

[20] Political Geography Glossary. http://www.umsl.edu / ~ naumannj / geog%202001%20glossaries / political%20geographyh / POLITICALL%20GEOGRAPHY%20GLOSSARY.doc (accessed January 13, 2009)

[21] U.S. Department of Defense. *Annual Report to congress, Military Power of the People's Republic of China*, (Washington, D.C: Department of Defense, 2007), 1

[22] Geoffrey Blainey, *The Causes of War* (New York: The Free Press, 1988), 3.

[23] Geoffrey Blainey, 3.

[24] Headquarters U.S. Marine Corps, Warfighting, MCDP 1 (Washington, D.C: U.S. Marine Corps, June 20, 1997), 3.

[25] Headquarters U.S. Marine Corps, *Marine Corps vision & Strategy 2025*, 2.

[26] United States Department of Defense, *2008 National Defense Strategy,13*.

[27] Michael R. Melillo, "Outfitting a Big-War Military with Small-War Capabilities," Parameters, US Army War College Quarterly (Autumn 2006): 22-23, Http:// www . Carlisle . army . mil / usawc / Parameters / 06autumn / melillo.htm (accessed January 10, 2009)

[28] Michael R. Melillo, 22-30.

[29] Michael R. Melillo, 34.

[30] Robert Gates, "Speaking at the Association of the United States Army," by US federal News Service and US State News, November 1, 2007, http:// proquest . umi . com / pqdweb?did=1395342881&Fmt = 3&clientId=32176&RQT=309&VName=PQD (accessed October 22, 2008)

[31] Robert Gates, "The National Defense Strategy Striking the Right Balance," Joint Force Quarterly, issue 52, (January 2009): 6.

[32] Donald P. Wright and Timothy R. Reese, *ON POINT II: Transition to the New Campaign: The United States Army in Operation Iraqi Freedom, May 2003 – January 2005* (Fort Leavenworth, KS: Combat Studies Institute Press, 2008), http: // www . globalsecurity . org / military / library / report / 2008 / onpoint / chap02-07.htm (accessed January 15, 2009)

[33] Donald P. Wright and Timothy R. Reese, *ON POINT II: Transition to the New Campaign: The United States Army in Operation Iraqi Freedom, May 2003 – January 2005.*

[34] Michael R. Gordon, "Fateful Choice on Iraq Army Bypassed Debate," *New York Times*, March 17, 2008

[35] Earl F. Ziemke, The US Army in the Occupation of Germany: 1944-1946 (Washington D.C: DA, Center of Military History, 1990), 23.

[36] James Dobbins, Andrew Rathmell, Keith Crane, Seth G. Jones, and John G. McGinn, "Japan," *America's Role in Nation building: From Germany to Iraq* (Santa Monica, CA: RAND Publications, 2005), 30 -40.

[37] Robert M. Gates, " A Balanced Strategy: Reprogramming the Pentagon for a new Age," Foreign Affairs, Vol. 88 Jan/Feb 2009, http: // proquest . umi . com / pqdweb?index = 0&sid=1&srchmode=1&vinst=PROD&fmt=3&st.... (accessed January 17, 2009)

[38] Robert M. Gates, " A Balanced Strategy: Reprogramming the Pentagon for a new Age,"

[39] Robert M. Gates, " A Balanced Strategy: Reprogramming the Pentagon for a new Age,"

[40] David Kilcullen, " New Paradigms for the 20th Century Conflict," ejournal USA: Foreign policy Agenda, US Department of State 12, 1 May 2007. http: // usinfo.state.gov / Journals / itps / 0507 / ijpe / kilcullen.htm, 39-45.

[41] David Kilcullen, 39-45.

[42] "Interagency and Political-Military Dimensions of Peace Operations: Haiti- A Case Study," 1996, National Defense University's, Center for Advanced Concepts and Technology. Http: // www . dodccrp . org / files / hayes _ Interagency. Pdf (Accessed January 20, 2009)

[43] Robert M. Gates, " A Balanced Strategy: Reprogramming the Pentagon for a new Age,"

[44] Sarah e. Kreps, "The 2006 Lebanon War: Lessons Learned," *Parameters*, (Spring 2007): 73-77, http: // carlisle – www . army . mil / usawc / Parameters / 07spring / kreps.htm (Accessed January 10, 2009)

[45] Sarah e. Kreps, 76.

[46] Matt M. Matthews, "We Were Caught Unprepared: The 2006 Hezbollah-Israeli War, Long War Series Occasional Paper 26 (Fort Leavenworth, KS: Combat Studies Institute Press, 2008), 61.

[47] Matt M. Matthews, 2.

[48] Matt M. Matthews, 1, 63.

[49] Matt M. Matthews, 21.

[50] General Makhmut Gareev, 45.

Bibliography

Appleman, Roy E. *United States Army In The Korean War SOUTH TO THE NAKTONG, NORTH TO THE YALU*. Washington D.C: Center of Military History United States Army, 1992.

Blainey, Geoffrey. *The Causes Of War*. New York: The Free Press, 1988.

Casey, George W. "U.S. Army Prepares for Future conflicts." *Military Technology*, Vol. 3. (October 2007): 18-21. http:// proquest.umi.com/.

Dobbins, James, Andrew Rathmell, Keith Crane, Seth G. Jones, and John G. McGinn. *America's Role in Nation building: From Germany to Iraq*. Santa Monica, CA: RAND Publications, 2005.

Gareev, Makhmut. *If War Comes tomorrow? The Contours of Future Armed Conflict*. London: Frank Cass Publisher, 1998.

Gates, Robert. "Speaking at the Association of the United States Army." *US Federal News Service and US State News* (November 1, 2007). http:// proquest.umi.com/.

Gates, Robert. "The National Defense Strategy Striking the Right Balance". *Joint Force Quarterly*, issue 52 (January 2009): 2-7.

Gates, Robert. "A Balanced Strategy: Reprogramming the Pentagon for a New Age". *Foreign affairs*, Vol. 88, Iss 1 (Jan/Feb 2009). http:// proquest.umi.com/.

Gordon, Michael R. "Fateful Choice on Iraq Army Bypassed Debate." *New York Times,*March 17, 2008. http:// www. nytimes .com/ 2008 / 03 / 17/world / middleeast/ 17bremer.html? pagewanted=1& _ r (accessed January 20, 2009).

Grenville, J.A.S. *A History of the World in the Twentieth Century*. Massachusetts: the Belknap Press of Harvard University Press, 1994.

Hayes, Margaret, Weatley, Gary F. "Interagency and Political-Military Dimensions of Peace Operations: Haiti- a Case Study," National Defense University's Center for Advanced Concepts and Technology. Http:// www . dodccrp . org / files / hayes _ interagency.pdf (accessed January 20, 2009).

Kilcullen, David. "New Paradigms for 20th Century Conflict." ejournal USA: Foreign Policy Agenda, US Department of State 12, May 1, 2007. http: // usinfo.state.gov / Journals / itps / 0507 / ijpe / kilcullen.htm.

Kreps, Sarah E. " The 2006 Lebanon War: Lessons Learned." *Parameters*, Spring 2007. http: // carlisle- www . army . mil / usawc / Parameters / 07spring / kreps.htm (accessed January 10, 2009).

Marine Corps Combat Development Command. *A Tentative Manual For Countering Irregular Threats An Updated Approach To Counterinsurgency*. Quantico, Virginia: Marine Corps, June 07 2006.

Matthews, Matt M. " We Were Caught Unprepared: The 2006 Hezbollah-Israeli War". *Long Series Occasional Paper 26*. Fort Leavenworth, KS: Combat Studies Institute Press, 2008.

Melillo, Michael R. " Outfitting a Big-War Military with Small- War Capabilities." *Parameters, US Army War College Quarterly*. (Autumn 2006): 22-35. Http:// www . Carlisle . army . mil / usawc / Parameters / 06autumn / melillo.htm. (accessed January 10, 2009).

U.S. Department of Defense. *Joint Publication 1-02: Department of Defense Dictionary of Military and Associated terms*. Washington, D.C: U.S. Department of Defense, October 17, 2008.

United States Department of Defense. *2008 National Defense Strategy*. Washington, D. C: U.S. Department of Defense, 2008. http:// www . defenselink . mil / news /2008%20national %20defense%strategy.pdf (accessed January 15, 2009).

U.S. Department of Defense. *Annual Report to Congress, Military Power of the People's republic of China*. Washington, D.C: U.S. Department of Defense, 2008.

U.S. Marine Corps. *Marine Corps Vision & Strategy 2025*. Washington D.C: U.S. Marine Corps, 19-23.

U.S. Marine Corps. *Warfighting MCDP-1*. Washington, D.C: Headquarters U.S. Marine Corps, August1, 1997.

U.S. Special Operations Command and Assistant Secretary of Defense for Special Operations and Low-intensity Conflict. *Summary of Irregular Warfare Workshop*. (September 20, 2005) http:// smallwars . quantico. usmc . mil / search / articles / Summary of Irregular Warfare Workshop.pdf (accessed January 14, 2009).

Wright, Donald P. and Timothy R.Reese. *On Point II: Transition to the New Campaign: The United States Army in operation Iraqi Freedom, May 2003-January 2005*. Fort Leavenworth, KS: Combat Studies Institute Press , 2008. http:// www. globalsecurity .org /military /library /report /2008 /onpoint /chap02-07.htm (accessed January 15, 2009).

Ziemke, Earl F. *The US Army in the Occupation of Germany:1944-1946*. Washington, D.C: Center of Military History, 1990.